A Dock At
The Bayman
Bay Club On
Guanaja
Island

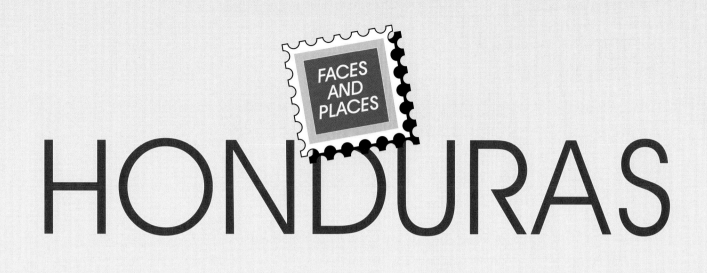

FACES
AND
PLACES

HONDURAS

BY PATRICK MERRICK

THE CHILD'S WORLD®, INC.

GRAPHIC DESIGN AND PRODUCTION
Robert E. Bonaker / Graphic Design & Consulting Co.

PHOTO RESEARCH
James R. Rothaus / James R. Rothaus & Associates

COVER PHOTO
Portrait of a Honduran boy
by: ©Charles & Josette Lenars/CORBIS

Library of Congress Cataloging-in-Publication Data
Merrick, Patrick.
Honduras / by Patrick Merrick.
p. cm.
Includes index.
Summary: Introduces the history, geography, people, and
customs of the Central American country of Honduras.
ISBN 1-56766-736-8 (lib. bdg. : alk. paper)

1. Honduras — Juvenile literature.
[1. Honduras.] I. Title.

F1503.2.M47 2000   99-38770
972.83 — dc21   CIP
                                                           AC

Table
of
Contents

ADMIT ONE   ADMIT ONE

When the astronauts first viewed Earth from space, they were impressed by how beautiful it was. From space, you can see that the planet is covered by huge oceans of water. Within these oceans, there are large areas of land called **continents**.

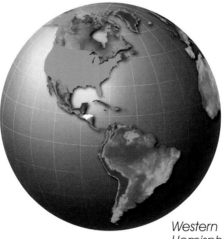

Western Hemisphere

Eastern Hemisphere

Both Honduras (white) And U.S.A. (green) Are In The West

In the southern part of the North American continent, there is a large area of land called **Central America**.

There are many fascinating countries in Central America. One of these countries is called Honduras.

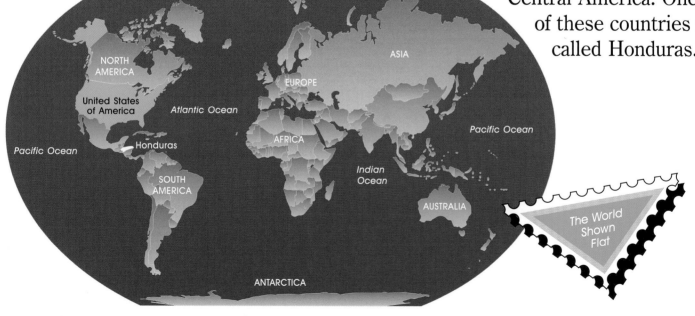

Arctic Ocean

NORTH AMERICA

United States of America

Atlantic Ocean

Pacific Ocean

Honduras

SOUTH AMERICA

EUROPE

ASIA

AFRICA

Indian Ocean

Pacific Ocean

AUSTRALIA

ANTARCTICA

The World Shown Flat

MEXICO

BELIZE

Caribbean Sea

GUATEMALA

HONDURAS

EL SALVADOR

NICARAGUA

*Pacific
Ocean*

COSTA RICA

ROATÁN ISLAND GUANAJA ISLAND

Gorgonian
Coral Off
Roatán
Island

The Land

While most of Honduras is nestled deep in the mountains, it also has many other types of places to live. There are swampy areas in the east and forests in the north. In between, there are open valleys, wide rivers, and blue lakes. Honduras has beaches on both it's Pacific and Caribbean coasts.

Off the coast of Honduras lies a series of beautiful islands. These islands are actually old volcanoes. They are now covered with tropical plants and white beaches. Also off the Honduran coast is the second largest coral reef in the world.

©Tony Arruza/CORBIS

A Waterfall On Guanaja Island

©Yann Arthus-Bertrand/CORBIS

Trees On Guanaja Island's Mountains Blown Down By Hurricane Mitch

A Buffon's Great Green Macaw Parrot On A Palm Tree Near Trujillo

©Tom Brakefield/CORBIS

Because Honduras has so many different types of land, it also has many different types of plants and animals. There are mangrove and swaying palm trees in the lowlands. High in the mountains, tall oak and pine trees grow. Most of Honduras is covered by forests. In fact, there are even thick tropical forests along the coasts.

A Bottlenose Dolphin In The Waters Off Of Puerto Cortéz

©Tom Brakefield/CORBIS

Each different area has wonderful and exotic animals. There are puma, fox, boars, and panthers in the mountains and brightly colored birds and snakes in the forests. There are even crocodiles and giant iguanas walking on the beaches of the rivers!

GUANAJA ISLAND

Puerto Cortéz • Trujillo

A Palm
Tree On
A Guanaja
Island
Beach

The Ruins Of
A Pyramid
In The
Ancient
Mayan City
Of Copán

∴ COPÁN RUINS

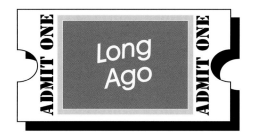
People have been living in Honduras for more than 8,000 years. Early people we call *Mayans* built large stone cities and temples. They built them so well that some of the temples are still standing thousands of years later!

Explorer Christopher Columbus (1451-1506)

© Bettmann/CORBIS

A Stone Face In The Ruins Of The Mayan City Of Copán

In 1502, Christopher Columbus landed on the beaches of Honduras. Soon after that, people from Europe came to Honduras looking for gold. For the next 300 years, the European country of Spain ruled the area. Finally, in 1838, Honduras became its own country.

Houses In The Town Of Guanaja Damaged By Hurricane Mitch

©Yann Arthus-Bertrand/CORBIS

For a long time, Honduras had troubles with fighting and **poverty**. Poverty is when people barely have enough money to live. Today, Honduras is still a very poor country. Many of its people live in small villages and grow just enough food to survive. The government is trying to help its people, and life is getting better for some Hondurans.

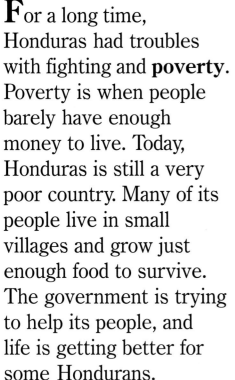

©Jim McDonald/CORBIS

A Family Home In "The Barrio" In Tegucigalpa

In 1998, a huge storm called Hurricane Mitch hit the country of Honduras. It was one of the worst disasters in the nation's history. The hurricane destroyed buildings and homes. It wiped away roads and entire villages. In fact, more than 10,000 people died! It will take a long time for Honduras to recover from this storm.

Guanaja

★ Tegucigalpa

• Choluteca

©Tony Arruza/CORBIS

Cholutecan People Who Lack Indoor Plumbing Washing Clothes In The River

A Woman
Carrying
Ducks And
Chickens
To Market

The People

Because the Native Indian people and the people from Europe have been living together in Honduras for so long, most Hondurans today are **mestizos**. This means they are part Indian and part European. While they are a very hard-working people, they are also very friendly and enjoy having fun.

The population of Honduras is getting bigger. There are a lot of young people living in Honduras. Most people there are under the age of twenty. In fact, four out of every ten people are children!

©Tony Arruza/CORBIS

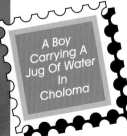

A Honduran Family Near San Pedro Sula

A Boy Carrying A Jug Of Water In Choloma

©Owen Franken/CORBIS

Thatched Houses In The Country

Most Hondurans live in the country. Here life is very hard. That is because most people must work long hours to grow an important crop —bananas. Because life is so hard in the country, many people are moving to the city.

©Macduff Everton/CORBIS

A Crowd Of People Cross An Intersection In Front Of A Church In Tegucigalpa

©The Purcell Team/CORBIS

In the big cities like Tegucigalpa (teh-goo-chee-GAHL-pah), life is more like it is in other cities of the world. However, so many people are moving to Honduras' cities, there is not enough clean water to drink and nice places to live.

18

O LOS COCHINOS ISLAND

★ Tegucigalpa

©Kevin Schafer/CORBIS

Houses In A
Miskito Indian
Village On
Los Cochinos
Island

A Girl
Drawing In A
Coloring Book In
A School In
Choloma

• Choloma

• Valle de Angeles

©Tony Arruza/CORBIS

A Baker Standing In A Bakery Doorway In Valle de Angeles

©Macduff Everton/CORBIS

In Honduras, children are required to go to school from age 7 to age 12. In school, they learn how to read and write and do math and science. They also have fun in school by playing games and singing songs. Many children don't go to school, however, because there are too few teachers and schools.

Children Attending Class In A Makeshift School In The Country

When you go to a city in Honduras, you will hear people speaking Spanish, the country's official language. If you go to the smaller villages, however, you can still hear people speaking the Native Indian languages their relatives spoke hundreds of years ago.

©Bill Gentile/CORBIS

Work

Most people in Honduras are farmers. Because of the nice weather, they can grow corn, beans, sugarcane, coffee, and bananas. There are many other jobs in Honduras, too. Along the coasts, fishermen catch lobsters and shrimp. In the mountains, workers cut down trees for wood and paper or work deep in mines looking for silver or gold.

In the cities, Hondurans find jobs in factories that make clothes or in restaurants or shops.

Workers Harvesting Bananas

©MacDuff Everton/CORBIS

Workers Carving Designs In Wood In A Factory In El Progreso

El Progreso

©Linda Richardson/CORBIS

Men
Fishing For Shrimp
On The North
Coast

Women
Making
Tortillas In A
Camp Near
Nacome

• Choloma
★ Tegucigalpa
• Nacome

©Owen Franken/CORBIS

A Woman Cooking Plato Típico In Choloma

©Tony Arruza/CORBIS

There are as many wonderful foods in Honduras as there are places to eat them. One of the most important foods is the corn **tortilla.** Tortillas are like flat pancakes and are served with a lot of meals. Besides corn, beans and rice are also found in most dishes.

Corn And Bananas On A Grill In Tegucigalpa

©Owen Franken/CORBIS

One dish that is a favorite of many people is *plato típico*. It is made of beef, pork, grilled peppers, onions, tomatoes, and many other things, all rolled into a tortilla.

If you would rather have seafood, Honduras has that as well. You can find seafood such as fish, shrimp, and lobster. In the larger cities, you can even get Italian or Chinese foods.

The people of Honduras love to play games. They like basketball, baseball, biking, and horse jumping. They also like to play golf and tennis, and go bass fishing in the famous Lake Yojoa. However, of all the sports that they play, there is no doubt which is the most popular. That sport is soccer. Children love to play it wherever they can, and everyone enjoys cheering on the most popular team—*El Olimpia*.

The people of Honduras celebrate many of the same holidays Americans do. They celebrate Christmas and Easter. They even have Columbus Day and Labor Day. A very special day for Honduras is their Independence Day (September 15).

Maybe someday you can visit Honduras. Then you can see the Mayan temples, walk along the white beaches, travel in the deep mountains, or watch a soccer game. Whatever you do, a trip to Honduras will be full of memories!

Boys On Lake Yojoa Holding Up Their Catch Of Fish

© Tony Arruza/CORBIS

COPÁN RUINS ∴ • Lake Yojoa
Santa de Rosa, Copán

©Tony Arruza/CORBIS

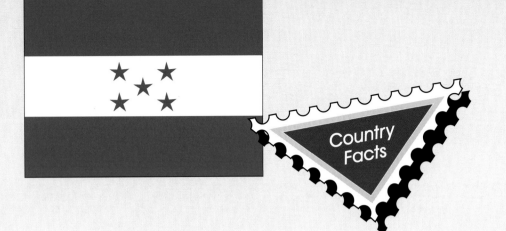

Area
About 43,000 square miles (112,000 square kilometers)—slightly bigger than the state of Tennessee.

Population
About 6 million people.

Capital City
Tegucigalpa.

Other Important Cities
San Pedro Sula, Puerto Cortés, and Choluteca.

Money
The Honduran lempira.

National Language
Spanish. There are also many Indian languages.

National Song
"Himno Nacional de Honduras," or "The National Anthem."

National Holiday
Independence Day on September 15.

National Flag
Two stripes of blue with a white stripe between them. The five small stars on the white stripe stand for Honduras and the other four original Central American countries.

Head of Government
The president of Honduras.

A Mayan
Jade Statue
From The
Copán Ruins

Honduras Trivia

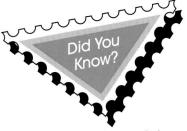

Did You Know?

A famous dance done in Honduras is called the punta. *It is a colorful and exciting dance where the dancers swerve and swing. It is performed to beautiful music.*

When Christopher Columbus saw the country for the first time, he noticed the deep ocean water off the coast. He then called the land "Honduras," which means, "depths."

One out of every four people in Honduras lives in the cities of Tegucigalpa and San Pedro Sula.

Hurricane Mitch was such a severe storm, it destroyed 70 percent of all the crops in Honduras.

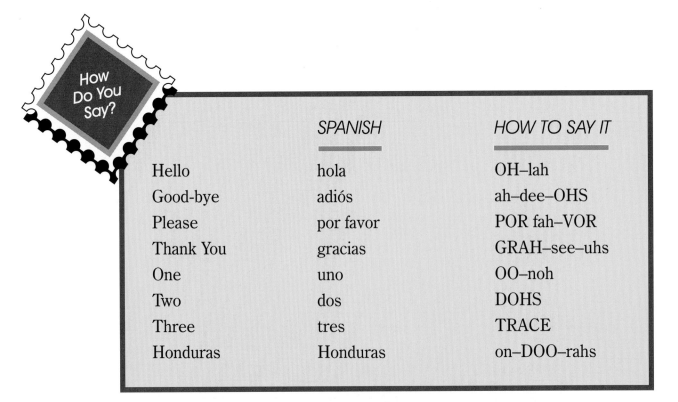

How Do You Say?

	SPANISH	HOW TO SAY IT
Hello	hola	OH–lah
Good-bye	adiós	ah–dee–OHS
Please	por favor	POR fah–VOR
Thank You	gracias	GRAH–see–uhs
One	uno	OO–noh
Two	dos	DOHS
Three	tres	TRACE
Honduras	Honduras	on–DOO–rahs

Glossary

Central America (SEN–tral uh–MARE–ih–kuh)
The lower part of North America that connects to South America is called Central America. Honduras is in Central America.

continents (KON–tih–nents)
Earth's large land areas are called continents. Honduras is a country on the North American continent.

mestizos (meh–STEE–zohs)
Honduran people who have both European and Native Indian backgrounds are called mestizos. Most Hondurans are mestizos.

poverty (PAH–ver–tee)
Poverty means being so poor that it is hard to find enough money for food and clothes. Many people in Honduras live in poverty.

tortilla (tor–TEE–yuh)
A tortilla is a flat pancake made of corn flour. Hondurans eat tortillas at almost every meal.

Index

Web Sites

Learn more about Honduras:
http://www.lonelyplanet.com/dest/cam/hon.htm
http://www.honduras.com

Learn how to say more Spanish words:
http://www.travlang.com/languages
(Then be sure to click on the word "Spanish.")

Learn how to make some Honduran foods:
http://www.hondurasinfo.hn/cuisine.html

Listen to the national anthem of Honduras:
http://www.emulateme.com/sounds/honduras.mid